alpha

science

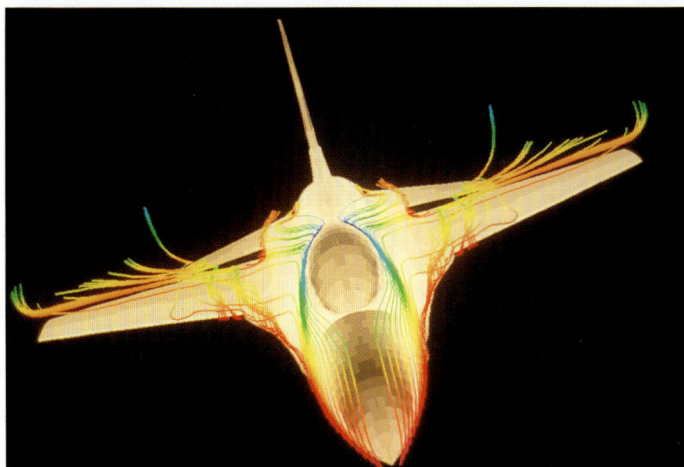

Movement

Isobel Smales

Evans   Evans Brothers Limited

This book is based on *Designs in Science Movement* by Sally and Adrian Morgan, first published by Evans Brothers Limited in 1993, but the original text has been simplified.

Evans Brothers Limited
2A Portman Mansions
Chiltern Street
London W1M 1LE

First published 1997

Printed in Hong Kong

ISBN 0 237 51772 8

Managing Editor: Su Swallow
Editor: Catherine Bradley
Designer: Neil Sayer
Typesetting: TJ Graphics
Production: Jenny Mulvanny
Illustrations: Hardlines, Charlbury
                David McAllister

Acknowledgements

For permission to reproduce copyright material the authors and publishers gratefully acknowledge the following:

Cover Michael Leach, Oxford Scientific Films
Title page Dayle Boyer, NASA/Science Photo Library
Contents page Sally Morgan, Ecoscene **page 4** (top) Robert Harding Picture Library (bottom) Sally Morgan, Ecoscene **page 5** Anthony Bannister, NHPA **page 6** Anthony Cooper, Ecoscene **page 7** (top) Sally Morgan, Ecoscene (bottom) Peter Parks, Oxford Scientific Films **page 8** (top) Ken Lucas, Planet Earth Pictures (bottom) Michael Melford, The Image Bank **page 9** Sally Morgan, Ecoscene **page 10** Sally Morgan, Ecoscene **page 11** (top) Peter Scoones, Planet Earth Pictures (bottom) Howard Hall, Oxford Scientific Films **page 12** Stephen Dalton, Science Photo Library **page 13** (top) Winkley, Ecoscene (middle) Rout, Ecoscene (bottom) Andrew Mounter, Planet Earth Pictures **page 14** Andy Callow, NHPA **page 15** Alastair Macewen, Oxford Scientific Films **page 16** (top) Dayle Boyer, NASA/ Science Photo Library (bottom and page 17) Stephen Dalton, NHPA **page 18** Stephen Dalton, NHPA **page 19** (left) Robert Harding Picture Library (right) Ben Osborne, Oxford Scientific Films **page 21** (top) Ken Lucas, Planet Earth Pictures (bottom) Manfred Danegger, NHPA **page 22** (top) Robert Harding Picture Library (bottom) Stephen Dalton, NHPA **page 23** (top) Schröter/Bildagentur Schuster/Robert Harding Picture Library (bottom) Sally Morgan, Ecoscene **page 24** (top) Gordon Maclean, Oxford Scientific Films (bottom left) Sally Morgan, Ecoscene (bottom right) Robert Francis, Robert Harding Picture Library **page 25** Stephen Dalton, NHPA **page 26** (left) Stephen Dalton, NHPA (right) Robert Harding Picture Library **page 27** (left) Robert Harding Picture Library (right) John Sanford, Science Photo Library **page 28** (top) Kevin Burchett, Bruce Coleman Ltd (middle) Lester, Ecoscene (bottom) Peter Menzel, Science Photo Library **page 29** (top) Dr David Jones, Science Photo Library (middle) Science Photo Library (bottom) Michael Klinec, Bruce Coleman Ltd **page 30** Sally Morgan, Ecoscene **page 31** TKM Automotive Ltd **page 32** (top) Gérard Lacz, NHPA (bottom) Stephen Dalton, NHPA **page 33** (top) Stephen Dalton, NHPA (bottom) Towse, Ecoscene **page 34** Hawkes, Ecoscene **page 35** Mike Devlin, Science Photo Library **page 36** Robert Harding Picture Library **page 37** (top) John Hayward, NHPA (bottom) Anthony Bannister, NHPA **page 38** (top) Stephen Dalton, NHPA (bottom) Towse, Ecoscene **page 40** Sally Morgan, Ecoscene **page 41** (top) Cooper, Ecoscene (bottom) Sally Morgan, Ecoscene **page 42** (top) Norbert Wu, Oxford Scientific Films (middle) Ron Church, Science Photo Library (bottom) Lockheed, Aviation Picture Library **page 43** Alex Bartel, Science Photo

Contents

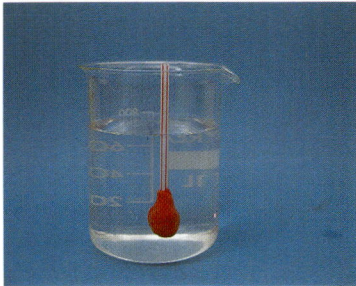

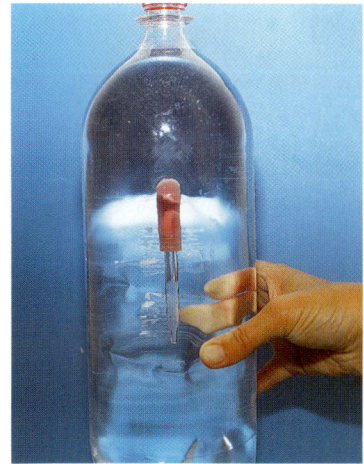

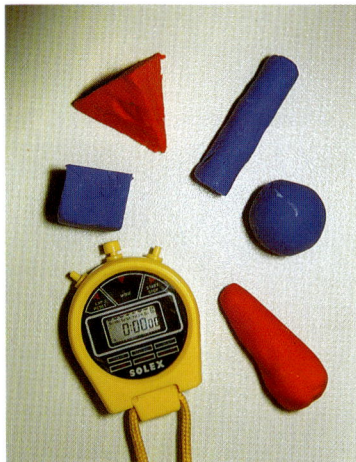

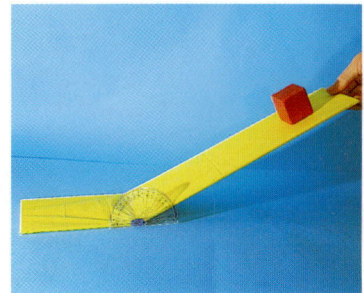

Concorde can fly faster than the speed of sound.

! *The fastest speed recorded for a bird is over 290 km/h, by a peregrine falcon that was swooping.*

Divers use flippers to push them through the water.

Introduction

There are many different ways to move. Birds and aeroplanes fly through the air. Fish and submarines move through water. Cats and cars move fast on land.

In nature, animals have many different features to help them move. When people design machines to move they often get ideas from living things. For example, the wings of most modern aeroplanes are specially shaped just like the wings of birds.

Why do things need to move? Animals move to find food and homes and to escape from danger. Plants need moving air and water to spread their seeds. They also need food and water to move up their stems from their roots to their leaves.

How does movement happen? An object stays still until a force is applied to it, which means until it is pushed or pulled. In other words, work has to be done to move an object. Work is done using energy. There are many forms of energy: movement energy, electrical energy, chemical energy and heat energy. Movement often involves changing one form of energy into another. When you run, you change chemical energy from your food into movement energy.

Moving on land, in air and in water

! *The world's fastest animals (birds) are found in the air. The world's largest animals (whales) live in the oceans.*

Measurement
In this book, some measurements are shortened:

Units of length
km kilometre
m metre
cm centimetre

Units of volume
cm³ centimetres cubed

Units of weight
kg kilogram
g gram

Units of time
h hour

The sidewinder moves its body in waves to cross the sand.

Moving on land is quite easy because the ground is solid. You can push against it to move. Moving through air and water is much more difficult because there is nothing solid to push against.

It is easier to move through air than through water. But water can support more weight, so larger animals can live in the water. Anything moving through air or water will feel a force against it, called resistance. The air or water has to be pushed out of the way, which slows the movement down. This resistance is called drag. Animals and machines that move overcome the problems of drag in different ways.

In this book you can find out how animals and machines move. In each section you will find some amazing facts, some experiments to try, and some questions for you to think about. At the end of each section, you will find a box called **Key words**. These boxes explain important words in the text. You can also look up difficult words in the Glossary on page 44.

Key words
Drag the resistance to movement. The flow of air or water over a moving object slows it down.
Resistance any force that slows movement down.

Moving in water

Well over half of our planet is covered by water. Many different animals live in water, from tiny bacteria to the largest living animal, the blue whale. Animals and machines that move on and under the water need to be able to float. They also need to have a smooth shape.

Floating and sinking

! *The water of the Dead Sea is so dense that you can float sitting up in it.*

Why does a steel ship float on the water while a solid lump of steel sinks? Floating and sinking involve density. If the object is more dense than the water it will sink. If it is less dense then it will float. The steel ship floats because it contains a lot of air, so it is less dense than the water. The solid lump of steel sinks because it is more dense than the water. Ships float at different levels in summer and winter, and at different levels in fresh water or sea water. This is because the density of sea water changes with its temperature and the amount of salt in it.

When something is put into water, the water pushes it up. If the object floats, we say it is buoyant.

Ships are carefully loaded so that they do not sink too deeply in the water.

? *Ships float at different levels in salt and fresh water. Will a ship float higher in salt or fresh water?*

EXPERIMENT

A simple hydrometer

You can compare the density of liquids using an object called a hydrometer. You will need: a drinking straw, some Plasticine, a large glass beaker or jam jar, some water and salt.

1. Make a simple hydrometer by cutting a 10 cm length of a drinking straw and putting a knob of Plasticine at one end.

2. Place the hydrometer in a beaker of water and check that it floats upright, as in the picture. You might need to change the amount of Plasticine.

3. Mark the straw with a pencil line level with the surface of the water.

4. Remove the hydrometer and add 10 cm³ salt to the water, stirring to make the salt dissolve. Put the hydrometer back in the salt water and make a new pencil line level with the water surface. Look at the two lines. Does the hydrometer float higher or lower in the water with the salt?

Depth control

Animals that live in the water need to be able to control how deep they go. Some animals, such as seals and whales, stay at the same depth for a short while by moving their fins or flippers. When they stop moving, they float upwards.

Using fins or flippers uses up valuable energy. Animals that need to spend a long time underwater do not need to use fins or flippers. They are neutrally buoyant. This means that the water pushing up on them is enough to keep them at the same depth.

Small sea creatures such as plankton have lots of bits sticking out of their bodies. This makes the surface of their bodies larger. They only sink very slowly in the water and can easily stay at one level by making small movements.

There are thousands of different kinds of plankton in the sea. They float easily by making small movements.

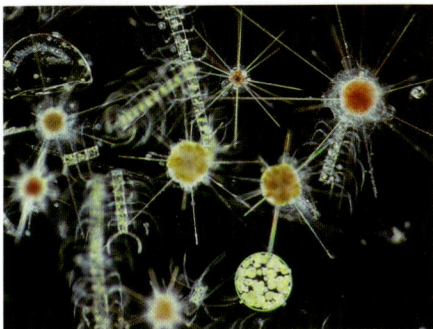

? *Can you think of any ways in which the tanks of a submarine are like the swim bladder of a goldfish?*

The nautilus (below) has pockets of gas inside its shell. It changes the amount of gas to move up and down in the water. The submarine (bottom) controls how deep it goes in the same way.

Fat and oil are less dense than water. Sharks have large, fatty livers which help to make them more buoyant, but they still have to swim all the time to stop themselves sinking.

Bony fish have a swim bladder, a small sack of air inside their body. They can change the amount of air in the bladder to change their buoyancy. Have you seen a goldfish gulping air in at the surface of the water? It is filling its swim bladder with air so that it can swim high in the water. To sink, it blows out bubbles of air.

People who design submarines get their ideas from underwater animals. Submarines have tanks that can be pumped full of air or be filled with sea water. When they are full of water, the submarine sinks. When they are

full of air, the density of the submarine is less than the density of the water, and the submarine rises.

EXPERIMENT

Buoyancy

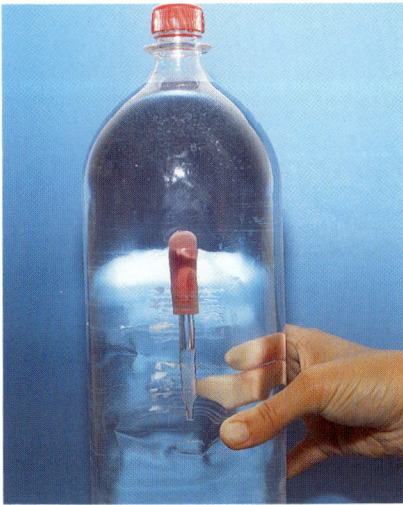

In this experiment you can see how pressure changes the buoyancy of an object. You will need: a 2 litre clear plastic bottle with a cap, an eye dropper and a tall glass beaker.

1. Fill the glass beaker with water.
2. Fill the eye dropper with enough water so that it floats in the beaker with its top only just above the surface.
3. Fill the bottle with water, and then very carefully put the eye dropper into the bottle. It is important that no water is lost from the dropper.
4. Screw the bottle cap tightly in place.
5. Squeeze the bottle. What happens to the dropper?

Explanation Squeezing the bottle increases the pressure of the water inside it. The air in the dropper cannot get out. The air is pushed into a smaller space, and more water enters. The dropper has less air, becomes denser and less buoyant, so it sinks. When you stop squeezing the bottle, the air can fill a larger space again and pushes the water back out of the dropper. This makes the dropper rise again.

Moving forward

A fish moves forwards by using the muscles along its back to make its body move in waves. This moves the tail and tail fin from side to side, which moves the fish forwards. Ships use propellers to move them forwards. Most large ships have a propeller with at least four blades. The blades force the water backwards and the ship moves forwards. The propellers are driven by machines called steam turbines.

Fish use their tail fin to move forwards. The other fins help them to swim straight, to steer and to balance. Ships have large fins called

! *The first ship to be driven by turbine, the* Turbinia, *appeared in 1897. It reached speeds of more than 60 km/h.*

dorsal fin

tail fin

ventral fin

pelvic fins (paired)

pectoral fins (paired)

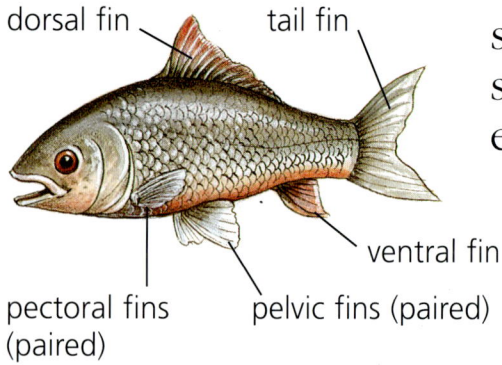

stabilisers below the water. These are used to stop the ship from rolling from side to side, especially in bad weather.

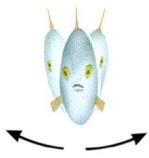

The dorsal and ventral fins stop the fish from rolling.

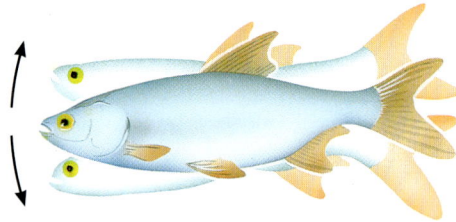

The paired fins (pectoral and pelvic) control movements up and down.

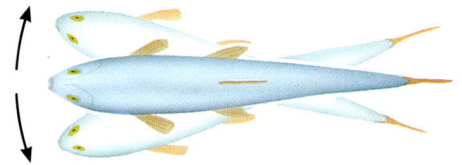

The dorsal and ventral fins also stop the fish moving from side to side.

Streamlined shapes

As an animal or machine moves through water it is slowed down by drag (see page 5). As it goes faster, there is more drag. It is very important for all animals that live in the sea to lower the effects of drag. Fish and other sea animals have found many different ways to solve this problem. One way is to have a

EXPERIMENT

Streamlining

In this experiment you can work out the best shapes for streamlining. You will need: a tall glass storage jar (the kind used for pasta), a little wallpaper paste, Plasticine and a stopwatch.

1. Fill the storage jar with wallpaper paste. This sticky liquid will slow down the movement of objects so that you can time how long they take to get to the bottom.

2. Divide the Plasticine into pieces that weigh about 20 g and make it into different shapes like the ones shown in the picture.

3. Using a stopwatch, record the time it takes for each object to fall from the top to the bottom of the cylinder. The object that is most streamlined will fall the fastest.

Which shape was the most streamlined? Which was the least streamlined?

? *How are a shark, a dolphin and a torpedo alike?*

Fish such as the barracuda (below) and mammals such as the dolphin (bottom) can move through the water fast because they are streamlined.

smooth, slippery shape. This is called streamlining. Streamlining is important for animals and machines both in water and when moving through the air.

Fish are pointed at each end, and have smooth surfaces, so the water flows easily around them. Their scales are covered with slimy mucus to make them very smooth. Fish need fins to control movement, but fins stick out from the body and make the drag worse. Some fish which have to swim fast to catch their food, such as tuna and barracuda, are very streamlined. They have very pointed snouts and smaller fins so that they can move very fast through the water.

Some mammals such as dolphins can also swim very fast underwater. They are well streamlined, and their skin is specially made with tiny ridges. These ridges help the water stick to the skin surface and make less drag.

People have copied some of the designs animals use to make less drag. Golf balls have tiny dimples in their surface like the ridges on the skin of the dolphin. This helps golf balls to fly more easily through the air.

! *The fastest animal in the sea is the sailfish, which can swim at 110 km/h over a short distance.*

The surface of a golfball and the skin of a dolphin both give extra speed.

Skimming the surface

Some animals live in water and air. They have to be able to move in both. Ducks, for example, have webbed feet for swimming and feathers for flying. Their feathers are covered with a natural oil to make them waterproof. Their streamlined body helps them to fly fast

The hydrofoil (above) and the hovercraft (right) are both designed to move across the surface of the water.

in the air and to dive fast underwater.

Flying boats have not yet been invented, but hovercrafts and hydrofoils skim over the surface of the water rather than push through it. This makes less drag. Hovercrafts and hydrofoils can travel at up to 80 km/h. A hydrofoil has small wings fixed to legs underneath it. It uses its propeller to start it moving, but once it is going quickly the wings lift it up off the surface of the water. The hovercraft rides on a cushion of air, so it can work on land as well as in the sea.

The Portuguese man-of-war is a jellyfish with gas floats which allow it to float right on the surface of the water. The floats are used like sails, catching the wind, which blows the jellyfish across the sea.

The float of the Portuguese man-of-war jellyfish is used like a sail to catch the wind.

Sailing with the wind behind
The sail is across the boat to trap the wind, which pushes the boat forwards.

Sailing into the wind
As the boat zigzags across the wind, the sail traps some of the wind to push the boat along.

Humans use sails on boats to trap the wind. Bigger sails catch more wind so bigger sails make the boat move more than smaller sails. If the wind is behind a boat, the sail is held across the boat to catch the wind. This pushes the boat forwards. If the wind is blowing towards the front of the boat, the boat has to travel in zigzags to catch the wind. This is called tacking.

? *In strong winds, sailing boats use smaller sails. Why do you think they do this?*

Surface tension

Surface tension makes drops of water form ball shapes.

Some small animals actually walk on the surface of water. These animals are denser than the water, so you would expect them to sink. They are supported by something called surface tension.

If you look at a drop of water such as a raindrop, it looks as if there is a skin holding the water in a ball shape. This is called surface tension. Water is made up of small particles called molecules. Water molecules are attracted to each other and they form bonds. The bonds are quite difficult to break,

Surface tension is surprisingly strong. It can support the weight of this large raft spider, which can grow up to 10 cm across.

so the water holds together. At the surface the molecules bond together to form a tight skin.

A number of small, light animals such as pond skaters use the surface tension of the water to move around. They have wax on the bottom of their feet so they can stand on the skin of water without breaking it.

? *What happens if you move a drop of water around on a flat surface, for example by pulling it along with your finger?*

Key words
Buoyancy being able to rise or float in water.
Density a measure of how closely the particles of a substance are packed together. Solids and liquids have a higher density than gases.
Streamlining the design of a smooth, slippery shape that makes less drag.
Surface tension force pulling the molecules in a liquid together, making the surface form a skin.

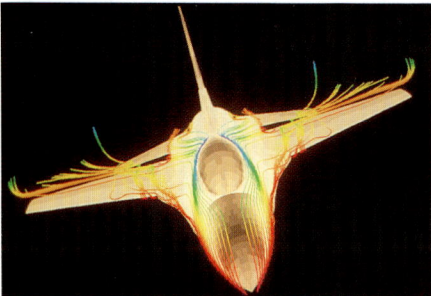

A computer picture of the flow of air over a jet aeroplane.

Taking to the air

Insects, birds and bats have been flying in our skies for millions of years. The first planes were invented less than 100 years ago.

Wing design

Patterns of air around a wing

The air below a wing moves more slowly than the air above it. This makes the air below the wing at a higher pressure than the air above it. The higher pressure of the air below the wing pushes the wing up. This is called lift. If the wing tilts, there is more lift. If it tilts too much, the air becomes rough. This is known as turbulence, and it slows the movement down.

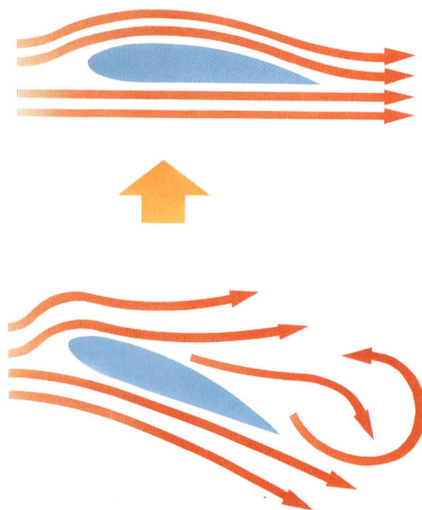

A little owl in flight. When the wings flap downwards the owl is pushed forwards.

To fly, an animal or machine must be able to lift itself into the air, and to move forwards. It must also be able to make the drag on its body less (see page 5), because drag slows it down. Flying animals and modern aero-planes fly using wings. All wings are the same basic shape, called an aerofoil. This shape gives the wings

EXPERIMENT

stream of air from the hair dryer

Design a wing

You will need: some thin card, a pencil and a hair dryer. Ask an adult for help if you need it.
1. Cut out a piece of card about 20 cm wide and 5 cm long.
2. Stick the two short ends of the card together as shown in the picture.
3. Hang the wing over a pencil.
4. Switch the hair dryer on to make a stream of air.
5. Hold the pencil in the stream of air. The wing will float upwards as in the picture.
Move the hairdryer closer to the wing, then further away. What happens?

! *Some dinosaurs could fly. Pteranodon had a wingspan of over 8 m, the size of a small plane.*

lift, which means that it helps them to rise up.

A bird's wing is designed to lift the bird in the air and move it forwards. It has different kinds of feathers, which help the bird to fly. Long feathers at the front of the wing help to push the bird forward. Behind these there are feathers that make the shape of an aerofoil, to give the wings lift.

Hummingbirds hover by flapping their wings very fast. The flapping makes a humming noise.

! *The world's smallest hummingbird, the bee hummingbird, weighs about 2 g and has a wingspan of less than 3 cm.*

A bird flaps its wings by using large muscles in its arms. The wings do not just flap up and down, but twist. This helps the feathers to push against the air and moves the bird upwards and forwards. Some small birds can also hover. To hover, birds flap their wings very quickly backwards and forwards (over 50 times a minute). Many big birds cannot flap fast enough to hover.

Most birds are quite small. Big birds are heavy so they need very strong arm muscles to flap their wings. Most big birds fly by gliding and soaring instead of flapping. Two birds, the ostrich and emu, are so heavy that they cannot fly. They move by running on their strong legs.

Gliding

Some birds can fly without flapping their wings. A man-made glider can fly without using an engine. This is called gliding. Gliders and gliding birds need to make a lot of lift so that they can stay in the sky. The best wings to have for gliding are long wings, which make the most lift.

In the sky, gliding birds and gliders can fly upwards in currents of warm air that rise up from the ground or sea. The wandering albatross uses warm air to glide over the sea. It has wings that are over 3 m across, which are very difficult to flap.

The albatross (below) and gliders (left) both have very long wings to help them to glide.

! *The albatross can glide for as long as six days without flapping its enormous wings at all.*

Special shapes for special jobs

Different birds have wings of different shapes. These help them to fly in different ways. Unlike aeroplanes, birds can change the shape of their wings. A bird can rise up in the air by stretching its wings out. It can swoop down by folding its wings back. Hawks fold their wings very close to their body, which helps them to dive down fast to catch their prey.

? *Look at the pictures of birds and planes below. What kind of flight do you think each one is designed for? Choose from:*
1. Long flights at high speed
2. Slow, gliding flight
3. Low-speed take-off with long slow flight
4. Fast flight which often changes direction.

A   B   C    D

Controlling flight

EXPERIMENT

Fly a slow roll

You can make a paper glider that will roll completely over while it is flying. You will need: some stiff paper and glue.

1. Take a piece of stiff paper and fold it in the way shown below.

2. Stick the sides of the main fold together.

3. If you fold the end of one wing up and the other down the glider will roll. Why do you think that bending the wings makes the glider roll?

1

2

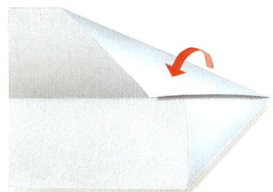
3

4

5

6

Changing direction

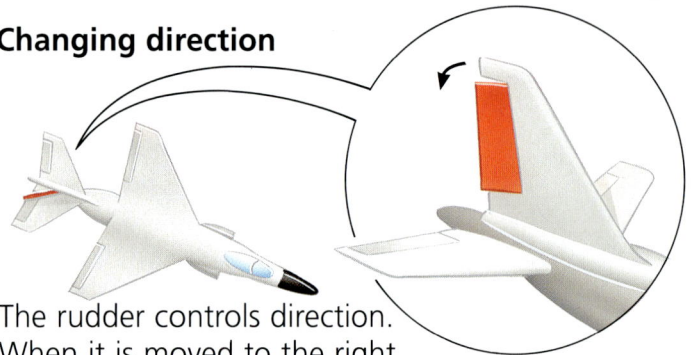

The rudder controls direction. When it is moved to the right, the plane turns right.

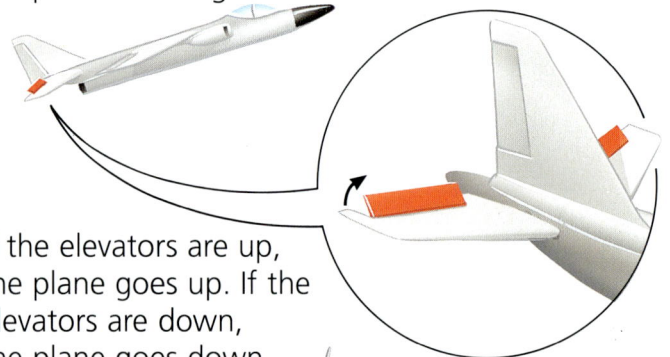

If the elevators are up, the plane goes up. If the elevators are down, the plane goes down.

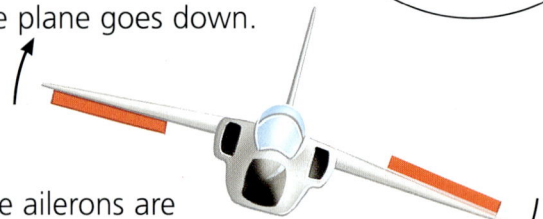

The ailerons are flaps used to make the plane roll from side to side. When one is up, the other is down.

Birds and aeroplanes can turn left and right and move up and down in the sky. To do this, aeroplanes have special flaps in their wings and tail. Birds use muscles to change the shape and angle of their wings and tail.

Powered flight

Most aeroplanes have engines to give them power and make them move. There are different kinds of engines. Aeroplanes which carry passengers usually have jet engines.
How does a jet engine work? If you blow

A modern jet engine

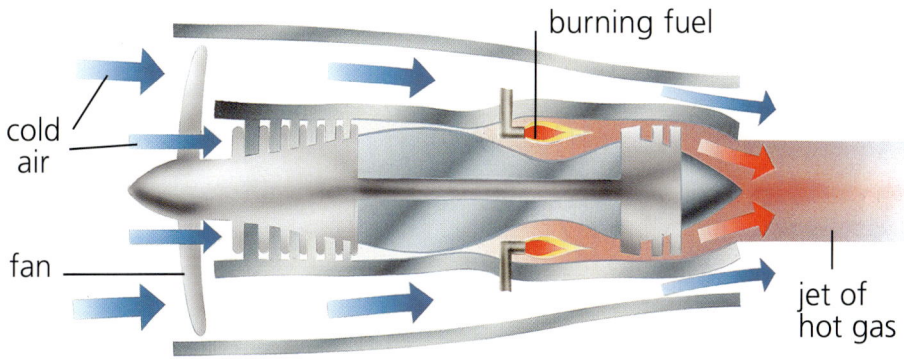

burning fuel

cold air

fan

jet of hot gas

Cold air is pulled into the engine by the fan. Some of the cold air is heated up. Fuel is sprayed into the hot air and the fuel burns. This makes hot gas. The hot gas and some of the cold air pushes out of the back of the engine, and the aeroplane moves forwards.

The squid uses a jet of water to move along.

up a balloon and let it go, the balloon will fly. This is because air escapes out of the hole at the bottom of the balloon and pushes the balloon along. A jet engine pushes hot gases out of the back of the engine. This pushes the engine along.

It is not just air that can push things along. Jets of water can also make things move. The squid moves by forcing water out of its body through a hole. This jet of water pushes the squid along.

Take-off and landing

A mute swan taking off

Small birds can take off from standing still. Larger birds run along to get enough speed to lift off the ground. Taking off from water is more tricky. Water birds such as swans use their large webbed feet to run across the surface of the water while they flap their wings. This helps them to get enough speed to take off.

Landing is more difficult. Birds have to slow down before they can land. They spread their wings out and make them point upwards. They also stretch out their legs. Water birds use their webbed feet as brakes.

? *Can you think of any ways in which a Harrier Jump Jet is like a squid?*

When a large aeroplane takes off the engines are at full power to give the plane a big push off the ground. It has flaps on its wings which can be moved out to make the wing bigger for more lift, so the plane climbs quickly.

A Harrier Jump Jet in flight

When landing, the aeroplane must slow down. The flaps are pointed upwards to make drag (see page 5), which slows the plane down.

Many aeroplanes need long runways to build up enough speed to take off. Some jets have special wings that help them to lift quickly at low speed. The Harrier Jump Jet can lift straight up in the air by using jets of gas from the engines which push downwards.

The structure of wings

! *The frigate bird has a wingspan of over 2 m, but its skeleton only weighs 125 g.*

Objects that fly must be very light and very strong. The skeleton of a bird and the frame of an aeroplane are built in a very similar way. They are both light, stiff and strong.

Honeycomb is very strong but very light.

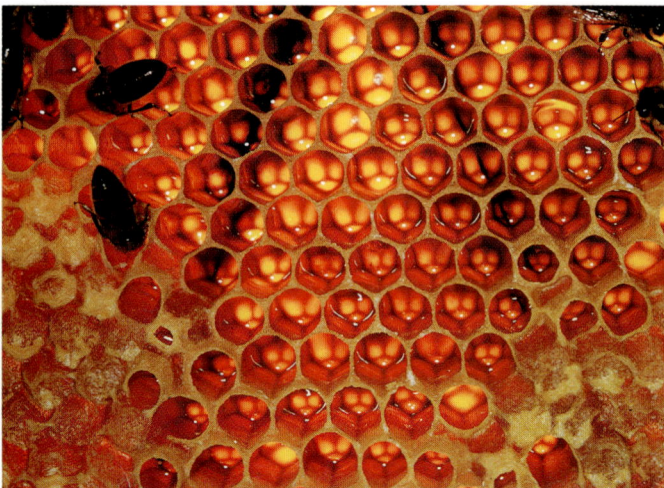

Birds have hollow bones, like tubes. They have big lungs, which are full of air. This makes birds very light. Aeroplane wings are hollow, just like a bird's bones. They are covered with a skin of thin metal. The frame of an aeroplane is made from material with a honeycomb shape, just like a bee honeycomb. Honeycomb is very strong but very light.

Parachutes and helicopters

People use parachutes to make them fall more slowly through the sky. As the parachute falls, the air pushes up against it and supports the person's weight. A parachute has an air hole at the top to let air pass through it. If there is no hole the air escapes from the edges. This makes the parachute swing from side to side.

Many plants have 'parachutes' on their seeds. The seeds are dropped into the wind and are carried away.

A person without a parachute falls ten times faster than a person with one.

EXPERIMENT

Make your own parachute

You will need: a square of cotton material, about 25 cm x 25 cm, some cotton thread and a small model figure (or a piece of Plasticine).
1. Cut four equal pieces of cotton thread, each about 50 cm long.
2. Tie one piece of cotton to each corner of the material, then tie all the other ends together.
3. Tie the model figure (or the Plasticine) to the knot you have just made.
4. Carefully fold the parachute with the figure inside it.
5. Throw the parachute into the air. Watch it open and fall to the ground.
Does it fall straight down? Does it swing from side to side?

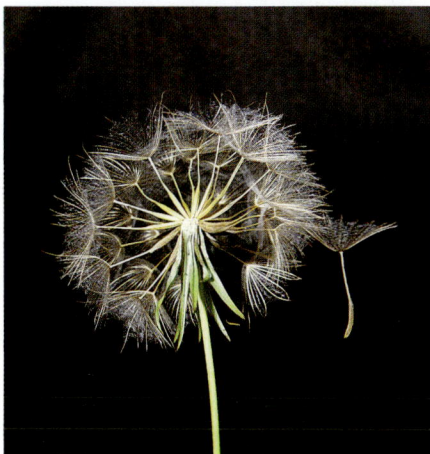

Many plants such as this dandelion have 'parachutes' on their seeds.

Pollen from the alder tree

Many flowers use wind to spread the male pollen to the female flower, so that seeds can be formed. Pollen grains are very light and can be carried for many kilometres in the wind.

A helicopter has blades which spin round to lift it off the ground. Each blade is wing-shaped. Many seeds spin like a helicopter when they fall. This slows them down. The sycamore has seeds like this.

Helicopters use spinning blades to lift them off the ground.

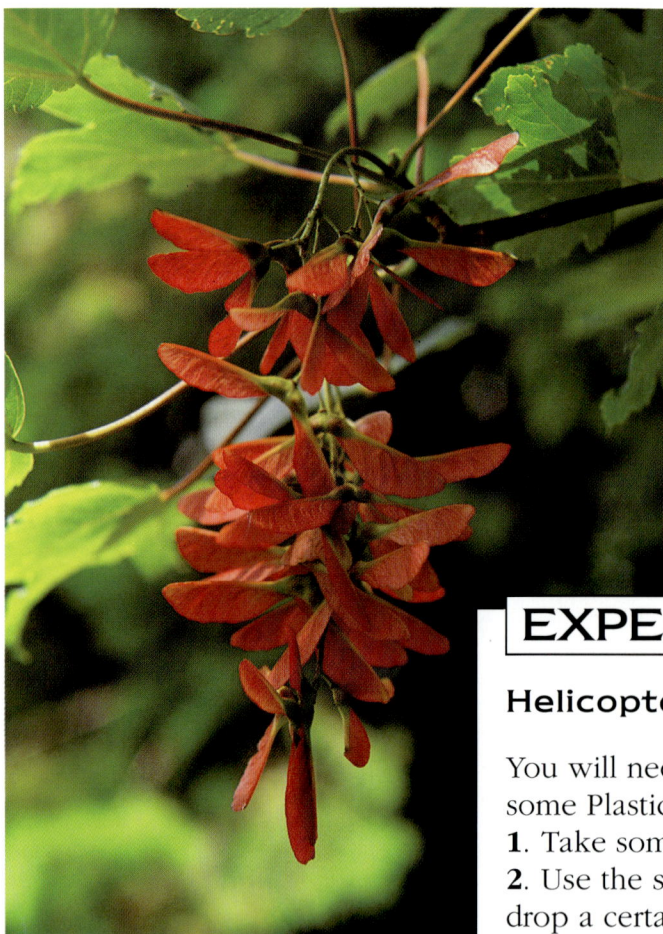
Sycamore seeds are in pairs. They spin like a helicopter as they fall.

EXPERIMENT

Helicopter seeds

You will need: some sycamore seeds, a piece of stiff card, some Plasticine and a stopwatch.
1. Take some sycamore seeds.
2. Use the stopwatch to time how long it takes for a seed to drop a certain distance, for example 2 m.
What happens if you break one of the double seeds in half and try again?
3. Using the card and Plasticine, try to make your own helicopter seed shape.

Insects and bats

The dragonfly has two pairs of wings, which flap. When the first pair of wings is flapping down, the second pair is flapping up.

Birds are not the only animals that can fly. Bats and insects can also fly. Birds, bats and insects all have wings that look very alike. But nature designed these wings in three different ways, so although they look alike, there are some differences.

Insect wings are unusual. They are made of a thin skin-like material called a membrane. Insect wings contain hollow veins instead of bones. The dragonfly is a large insect. It flies very strongly. It can also glide. Smaller insects cannot glide. They have to flap their wings all the time to stay in the air. Some insects beat their wings up to 1000 times each second.

A bat wing is also very different from a bird wing. It is made of a thin layer of skin. The skin stretches across the bat's arm and finger and joins its back leg. Like a bird, a bat has thin and light bones. A bat can change the speed it is flying by making the skin of its wings tighter or looser.

People have copied the wings of bats and birds to make hang-gliders. These are very light in weight. The wings are formed from a thin sheet of material stretched across a frame of hollow metal tubes.

The wings of bats and hang gliders are alike. They both have a thin skin stretched over a light frame.

Lighter than air

? *How do you think a balloon moves up and down in the sky?*

Hot air balloons are made of a huge pocket of lightweight material attached to a basket. There is a gas burner underneath the pocket to heat the air in the balloon. The heat makes the air get bigger and become less dense. The hot air inside the balloon is lighter than the surrounding air and the balloon rises up.

Some gases, such as helium, are lighter than air. A balloon filled with helium will easily lift into the sky, but the balloon must be sealed to stop the helium escaping.

The problem with balloons is that you

! *Richard Branson and Per Linstrand were the first people to cross the Atlantic Ocean by hot air balloon, in July 1987.*

Hot air balloons (below) and airships (below right) both need gas to provide lift.

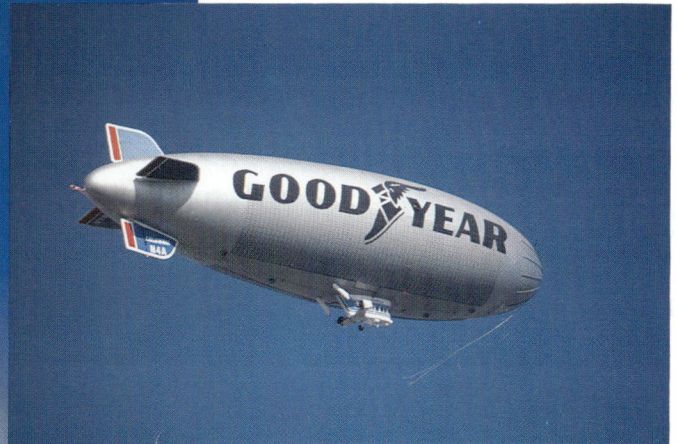

cannot steer them. They go wherever the wind blows them. But you can steer an airship. Airships are usually much bigger than hot air balloons. They are cigar-shaped, and filled with helium. They are moved along by propellers at the back. These propellers can also be used to steer them. The engines are the heaviest part of an airship. Everything else is made of very lightweight materials. Airships can stay up in the air for a long time.

! *The first airships were filled with hydrogen gas, but this burns in air and some of the early airships exploded. Helium does not burn in air, so it is quite safe to use it in airships.*

Key words
Aerofoil wing shape that cuts through air and makes lift.
Lift the force of air upwards that makes an object rise into the air.

Moving on land

Nearly all animals that live on land move using jointed arms or legs. Muscles make the arms or legs push backwards against the land. This makes the animal move forwards.

Most machines that move on land use wheels. No animals have wheels. Wheels are very useful for moving on flat surfaces. Jointed limbs like arms and legs can do more than this. They let animals climb trees and even mountains, which a vehicle with wheels cannot do. So it is better for animals to have jointed limbs than to have wheels.

Although limbs and wheels are very different, the same forces affect the way they work. The most important forces are gravity and friction. Animals and machines that move very fast can also be affected by air resistance.

△ Many machines use wheels to move on land, but they cannot move over all surfaces.

▷ Squirrels can run, climb and jump

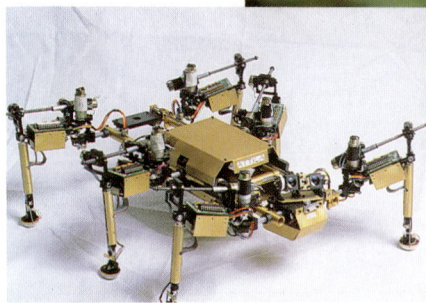

◁ This robot looks like an insect. It has jointed legs and can move over bumpy surfaces.

Gravity

All objects are attracted towards each other by a force called gravity. A larger object has a stronger gravitational pull than a smaller object. Gravity is quite weak, and objects have to be very large before its effects can be felt. There is a gravitational pull between two people standing next to each other, but it is so weak that you cannot feel it. The planet earth is so huge so that it has a large gravitational pull. This pull is strong enough to hold us on the ground. It is the force of gravity that keeps the moon in orbit around the earth, and the earth in orbit around the sun.

If we drop something, it falls to the ground. This is because it is pulled by the force of gravity towards the earth.

Friction

Why do gymnasts rub powder on their hands before they work on bars or rings?

When two surfaces rub together, they create a force called friction. Friction makes the movement more difficult. Try pushing a rubber across a table. If you press harder on the rubber, the rubber is harder to move. This is the force of friction.

It is harder to rub two rough surfaces together than two smooth ones. This is because there is more friction between the rough surfaces. But even if the surfaces are very smooth, there is still some friction.

We need friction in many of the things we do every day. If there was no friction between the tyres of a car and the road, the wheels would spin round out of control.

△ Even very smooth surfaces look very rough under a microscope. This is the surface of a piece of sticky paper.

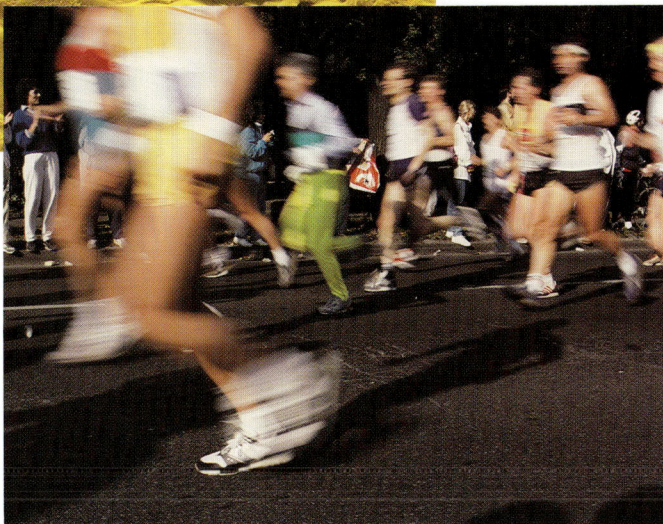

◁ Runners need friction to stop them from slipping.

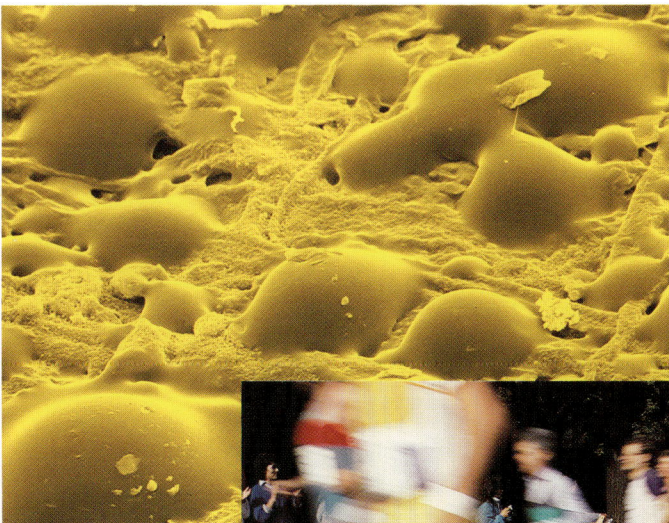

When a car uses its brakes, friction is produced which slows the car down. Friction helps to stop our feet from slipping when we walk. Friction also helps things to stay in place when we put them down.

In machinery, friction wastes power and damages the parts that move and rub together. One way to stop moving parts from rubbing is to put oil or grease between the two surfaces. This helps them to slide over each other more easily.

EXPERIMENT

Looking at friction

You will need: two pieces of plywood, some strong sticky tape, some felt and a sheet of plastic to cover the plywood, a small block of wood, some Blu-tack and a protractor.

1. Join the two pieces of wood together using strong sticky tape.

2. Cover the wood with the felt.

3. Stand the protractor next to the join between the two pieces of wood and stick it in place using some Blu-tack. Lift one piece of wood so that the angle of the slope measures 10 degrees on the protractor.

4. Place the block of wood at the top of the slope. Does it move?

5. Increase the angle of the slope slowly until the block moves. What angle is the slope when the block begins to move?

Try the same experiment again, this time using the plastic to cover the wood. Does the block slide down the slope more easily when it is covered in plastic? Does the plastic produce more or less friction?

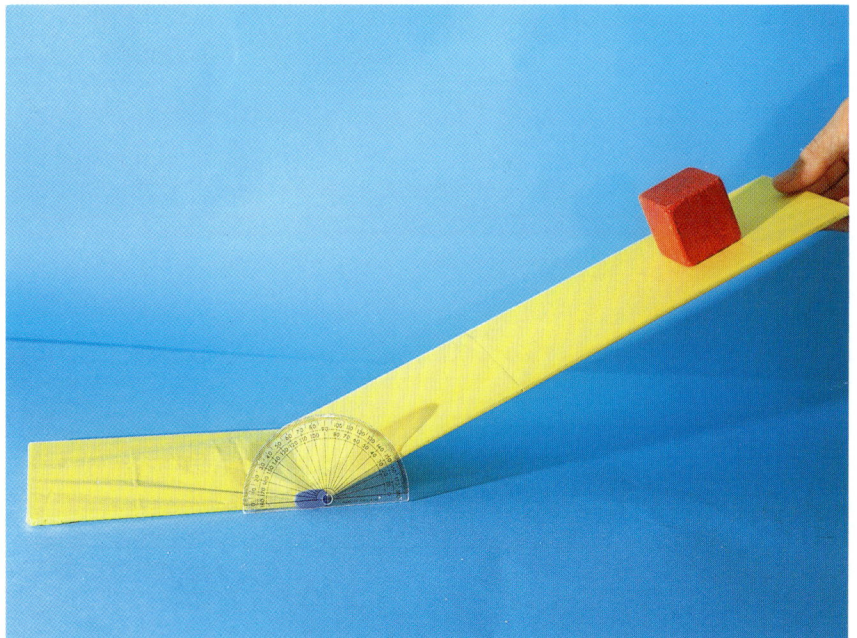

Air resistance

The cheetah can run faster than any other animal on land. How does its shape help it to run at high speeds?

As we have seen, friction makes it harder for things to move. There is even friction between a moving object and the air around it. This friction slows down movement through the air,

This car has a very streamlined shape.

and is called air resistance. The faster an object moves, the greater the air resistance.

Any person who is running will be slowed down by air resistance. To go faster, sprinters wear tight body suits. These produce much less air resistance than normal T-shirts and shorts. Air resistance does not have very much effect at walking speeds. Most animals move at walking speeds most of the time so they do not need to worry about air resistance.

Air resistance also slows down cars which are moving quickly. The best shape for a car to be is streamlined (see page 10). Air flows more smoothly over a streamlined car. Grand Prix racing cars have a low, smooth, streamlined shape so that they can go at very fast speeds.

Elastic forces

Some objects change shape when they are stretched or squashed. If an object goes back to the same shape again when the stretching or squashing stops, we say that it is elastic. A rubber band is elastic. So is a spring. An elastic object is said to recoil when it goes back to its original shape.

There are springs in a car. When a car goes over bumps in the road the springs squash up.

The kangaroo has very elastic tendons in its back legs which help it to jump.

! *The Klipspringer, a small South African antelope only 50 cm tall, can jump 10 m up a cliff face.*

The tree frog uses powerful leg muscles to push it forwards as it jumps.

Once the car is over the bumps they spring back into shape. This makes the car travel more smoothly.

The muscles and tendons (which join muscles to bones) in the

EXPERIMENT

Knee bends

Movement is helped by the elastic parts of our body recoiling into shape. This simple exercise will show you how.

1. Stand up with your feet together.
2. Slowly bend your knees, keeping your back straight, until your hands touch the floor next to you.
3. Stay like this for a few seconds, then stand up.
4. Do steps 1 to 3 nine more times.
5. Take a brief rest.
6. Do steps 1 to 4 again, but this time do not stop at the bottom of each bend. Is it easier with or without stopping?

If you do not stop at the bottom of each bend the tendons and muscles in your legs recoil back into shape, which helps you to bounce up again.

bodies of animals are also elastic. Kangaroos can jump well because their back legs have very long tendons which act like gigantic rubber bands, stretching and recoiling each time the kangaroo jumps.

Fleas and grasshoppers can jump over 50 times their own body length. Fleas have an elastic material like rubber at the bottom of their back legs. The flea uses its muscles to squash the rubber then let it go, which catapults the flea into the air.

Grasshoppers have very long back legs which are ideal for jumping.

If a click beetle lands on its back, it springs into the air with a loud clicking noise until it lands the right way up. It can spring up over 30 cm. How does it do this? On its back, it has a peg which is held flat. When the beetle is on its back, it lets the peg spring out like a little hammer. The peg hits the ground and throws the beetle up into the air.

When someone is running, their feet hit the ground very hard. This can lead to injuries. Running shoes are designed with elastic material in the sole. The elastic material stops the runner's feet from hitting the ground so hard.

Modern running shoes have pockets of air in the soles. These act as a cushion for your feet.

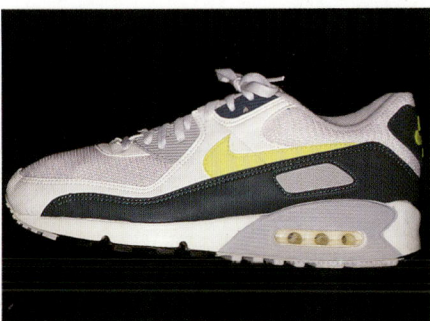

Levers

If you had to loosen a nut, would it be easier with a spanner with a long handle or a short handle?

Crowbars, scissors, nutcrackers and wheelbarrows all help us to carry out a task. They are all levers. The bones in our bodies are also levers. A lever is a bar that is fixed at one point. If you push or pull on the bar, it moves around the fixed point, which is called the fulcrum. We use levers for many different jobs. Levers can change a small force into a larger one. For example, you do not have to push very hard on a crowbar to move a heavy load a short distance. The longer the crowbar, the easier it is to move the load.

There are three kinds of levers. Class one levers are the most efficient. Scissors and crowbars are class one levers. Nutcrackers and wheelbarrows are class two levers. Class three levers are the least efficient. The human forearm is a class three lever.

A lever is used to move the rudder which steers this barge.

The three different kinds of lever

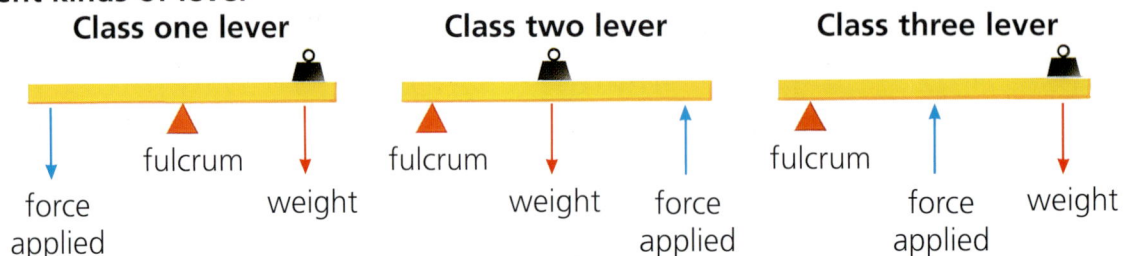

Class one lever	Class two lever	Class three lever
force applied — fulcrum — weight	fulcrum — weight — force applied	fulcrum — force applied — weight

EXPERIMENT

The seesaw

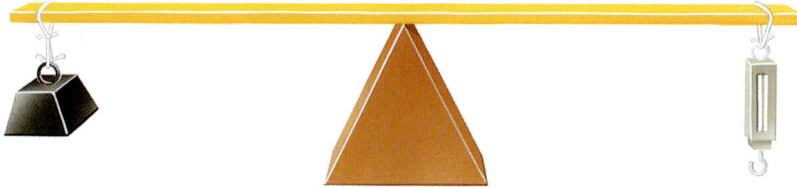

You will need: a long ruler, different weights, a small spring balance and a triangular piece of wood.
1. Set up the seesaw as shown in the picture. Attach a weight at one end and the spring balance at the other.
2. Attach weights to the spring balance to measure how much force has to be applied to lift the weight. Move the balance nearer the fulcrum. Is it easier or more difficult to lift the weight now?

Joints in animals

If people have damaged joints these are sometimes repaired with plastic or metal ones.

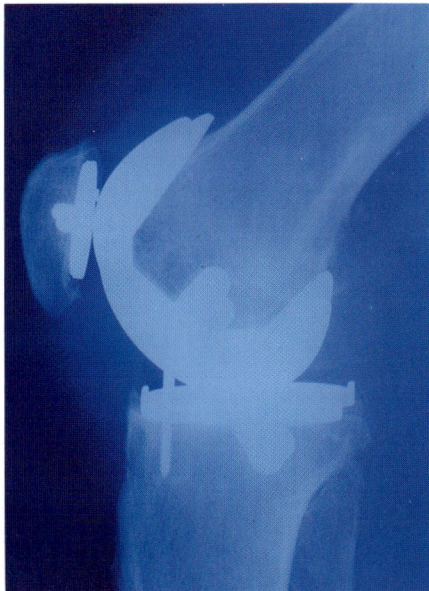

Key words
Friction The force that makes movement more difficult when two surfaces rub together.
Gravity The attraction between two objects. Gravity holds us down on the earth.
Elastic An object is said to be elastic if it goes back to its original shape after it has been stretched or squashed.

In animals, a joint is formed where two bones meet. Animals need joints to move. There are three main kinds of moving joint. The first kind is a ball-and-socket joint. The top of one bone is like a ball and fits into a space in the other bone (the socket).
Your shoulder and hip joint are ball-and-socket joints. The second kind is a hinge joint. Your elbow and knee are hinge joints.
The third kind of joint can only move a little. Your backbone has the third kind of joint.
Joints can be damaged by wear and tear. Many older people get a disease called arthritis in their joints. The joints swell and stiffen up, and are very painful. Arthritis is common in hips, knees and fingers. Badly damaged joints can be replaced with plastic or metal ones.

Liquids and pumps

Hydraulics at work

Hydraulic systems are used in heavy machinery. The arm of this digger is worked by pushing on the liquid in the tubes.

Hydraulic systems involve the movement of liquids in pipes. They work because liquids cannot be squashed into a smaller space. If two pistons of the same size are joined by a pipe, and filled with a liquid, pushing one piston in will make the other one push out by the same amount.

Hydraulic systems are used in many machines. A car's brakes are a hydraulic system. When the car driver presses the brake

EXPERIMENT

Copying a braking system

You will need: four small syringes and one large syringe, some rubber tubing, and a few T pieces to join the tubing.
1. Join the syringes and the tubing together as shown in the diagram.
2. Fill the system with water using the large syringe, keeping the plungers of the four small syringes fully in.
3. Push the plunger into the large syringe. What happens to the plungers of the four small syringes? Why does this happen?

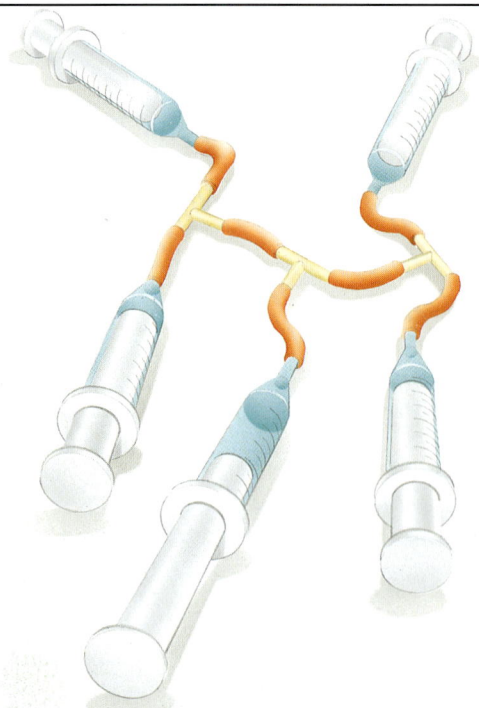

? *Why is it important that there are no air bubbles in a hydraulic system?*

pedal, it pushes a small piston. This pushes four bigger pistons. Each of these bigger pistons brakes one of the car's wheels.

Hydraulic systems are very powerful, but easy to control, so they are useful for doing heavy work such as building roads.

Hydraulics in animals

Hydraulic systems are used by many animals. Spiders use hydraulics to stretch their legs out. Their legs are full of liquid. They use the muscles in their body to press on the liquid which pushes out their legs. If a spider is hurt or dies, it cannot press on the liquid, so its legs curl up.

Starfish move by using hundreds of tiny tube feet. The tube feet are filled with liquid and

The starfish has hundreds of tiny tube feet which it pushes out by squeezing liquid into them.

The earthworm moves by pushing on the liquid inside its body.

can be pushed out by pressing on the liquid.

Have you ever watched an earthworm move? They use hydraulics too. They push the front part of their body along, then pull the back part up after it. They do this by using the muscles in the outer part of their body to push on the liquid inside their body.

Pumps

In a screw pump, a handle is used to turn the screw. As the screw turns, it moves water from the bottom of the screw to the top.

Pumps are used to move liquids from one place to another. Your heart is a pump, moving blood around your body.

A pump can make the liquid flow more strongly, and it can also lift the liquid up to a higher level. Pumps need power such as a motor or muscle to make them work.

People have been using pumps for about five thousand years. Early farmers used them to pump water up from wells under the ground to water their crops.

A lift pump

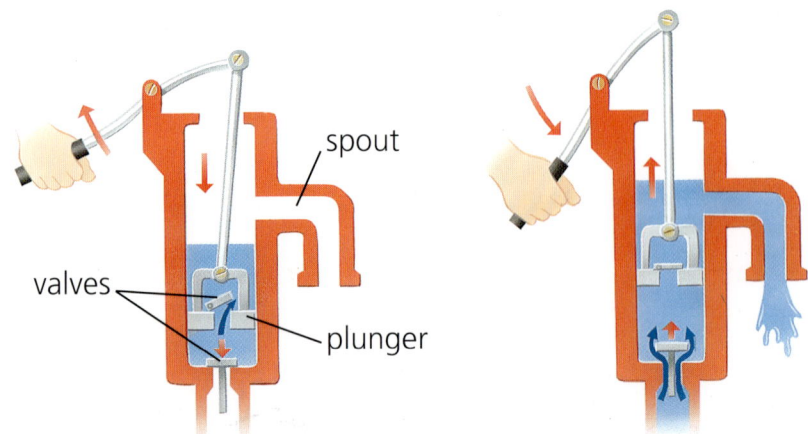

A lift pump is used to lift water up to a higher level. When the plunger is pushed down, the water shuts the valve at the bottom of the pump and opens a valve at the top. This lets water in above the plunger. When the plunger is pulled up, the top valve closes and water flows out of the spout. At the same time, the bottom valve opens and more water is pulled up.

The heart, a natural pump

! *A human heart will beat over 2000 million times in its lifetime.*

The human heart

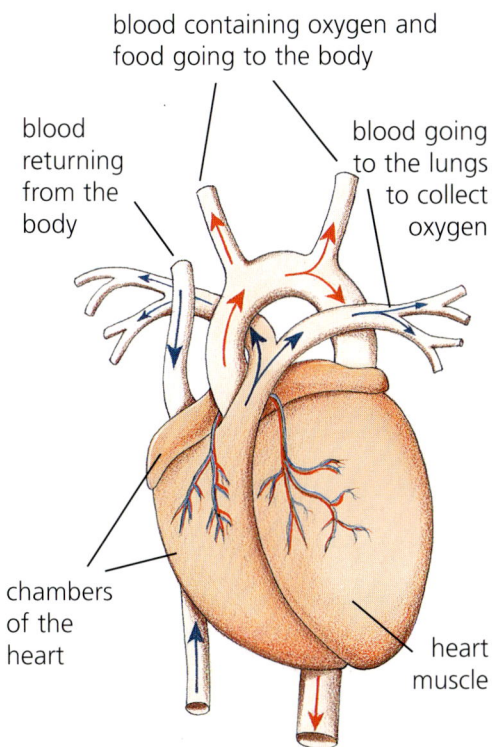

blood containing oxygen and food going to the body

blood returning from the body

blood going to the lungs to collect oxygen

chambers of the heart

heart muscle

Many animals have a heart. Insects and worms have very simple hearts, but mammals such as humans have very complicated hearts.

Why do you need a heart? Your heart pumps the blood around your body, in tubes called blood vessels. Your blood carries your food and the air that you breathe (oxygen) to the different parts of your body. If you exercise, your body needs more oxygen, so your heart has to pump faster.

EXPERIMENT

Taking your pulse

You will need: a stopwatch or a wristwatch with a second hand.
1. Sit down and rest for a few minutes, then take your pulse. Feel for your pulse on your wrist or on the side of your neck just under your jaw. Count how many beats you can feel in 20 seconds.
2. Now get up and run around for two minutes, then take your pulse again straight away.
Is your pulse rate faster or slower after you have run around?

? *Would you expect your heart to beat faster or slower than an adult's?*

How does the heart work? It is made of muscle. There are four spaces, called chambers, in the heart, two on each side. Blood from the body flows into the top chambers of the heart.

EXPERIMENT

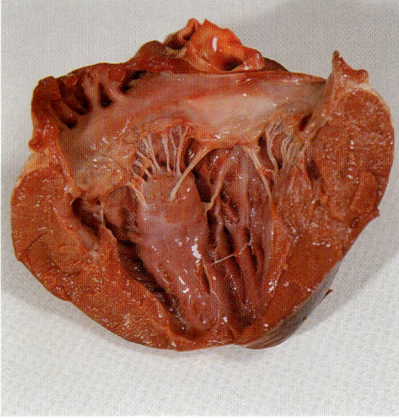

Looking at a heart

You will need to buy a sheep or pig heart. Most butchers and supermarkets sell them. You will also need: a chopping board and a pair of scissors. Ask an adult for help if you need it.

1. Look carefully at the outside of the heart. Can you see the blood vessels going into the top of the heart? They look like rubber tubes.

2. Using a pair of scissors, carefully cut through the wall of the heart and have a look inside. Can you see the big chambers at the bottom of the heart?

When these chambers are full of blood, the muscles around the top chambers contract (get smaller) and push the blood into the bottom chambers. Then the muscles around the bottom chambers contract, pushing the blood out of the heart and around the body. It is the muscles contracting that we can feel as a heart beat.

An adult's heart beats about 65-70 times every minute. Smaller mammals such as mice have much faster heart rates, about 200 beats every minute.

Movement in tubes

If you put some water in a very thin glass tube, the water will rise up the tube. The thinner the tube, the higher the water moves. This is called capillarity. You can see capillarity working when you use a paper towel to soak up water. The water creeps up between the fibres in the towel.

Water is made up of small particles called molecules. Capillarity happens because the water molecules near the edge of a tube are attracted to the sides of the tube. This pulls them upwards. Capillarity is very important for plants. Plants need to move water up from their roots to their leaves. The water travels up tiny tubes inside the plant stem by capillarity.

! *Over 200 litres of water can travel each day from the roots of an oak tree to its leaves.*

EXPERIMENT

Water on the move

This experiment shows capillarity in plants. You will need: a white flower like a daisy or carnation, some food colouring and a beaker of water.

1. Add a few drops of food colouring to the water in the beaker.

2. Place the stem of the flower in the coloured water and leave it for a few hours. When you come back you should see that the colour has been carried up to the petals. They will look stripy, like they do in the picture. The next experiment helps you to see the tiny tubes in the stem that carry the water.

3. Take a piece of celery and put the cut end in coloured water. Leave it for an hour, then remove it.

4. Ask an adult to help you cut the bottom 2 cm off. Can you see where the coloured water has travelled up the tubes in the stem?

The giant sequoias are the tallest living trees. They can grow to 100 m tall. Water has to be carried from the roots to the highest leaves.

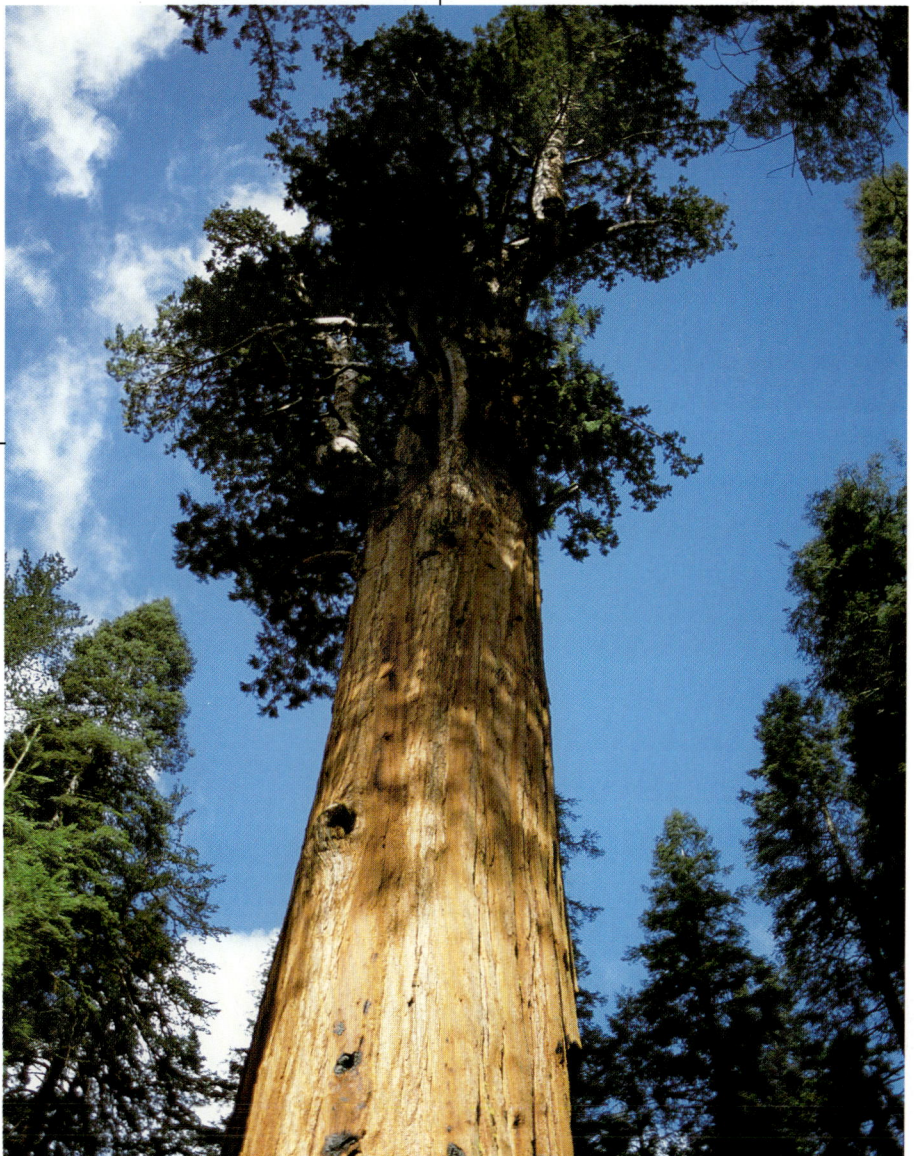

Key words

Capillarity when water rises up a tube because the water molecules are attracted to the sides of the tube.

Hydraulic system a system that works by moving liquid in pipes.

Pump a machine used to move liquids from one place to another.

Valve a structure that lets liquid flow only one way.

The future

We can be certain that people will develop even better and faster ships, aeroplanes and cars in the future.

The only parts of the world that people cannot travel to are the ocean depths. Strange animals are known to live deep in the oceans, but people have not yet designed a vehicle that can work at great depths for very long. As we use up more and more of the natural resources on land, people are looking for resources such as oil and gas in the sea. Divers cannot survive in the very deepest oceans, so people are designing vehicles driven by robots to collect oil and gas at great depths.

In the air, new materials are being used to build stronger and lighter aeroplanes. Although most aeroplanes have a very streamlined shape (see page 10), the latest Stealth fighters are not very streamlined. They have flat, sloped surfaces, to stop them being seen by radar. Jumbo jets can carry up to 400 passengers, but people are

Many fish like this fangtooth (above) can survive at great depths in our oceans. A submersible (right) can only reach depths of 1300 m. The deepest parts of the ocean go down to 11,000 m.

The Stealth fighters are not very streamlined, but they are designed to be invisible to radar.

developing aeroplanes that can carry up to 700 passengers. Other scientists are designing a supersonic plane which flies at the very top of the Earth's atmosphere. It is powered by a rocket engine, and will be able to fly to Australia in just 5 hours, instead of 20 hours.

On the sea, boats that carry passengers are being designed to go faster and more smoothly. The Japanese are designing a cross between a boat and a plane, which will travel a few metres above the surface of the waves.

On land, vehicles are being made to use less fuel and to make less pollution. Electricity is being used to power more vehicles such as trams and high speed trains.

There are many changes in the way we deal with problems with human movement too. In surgery, new materials and computer designs are helping to make better replacement joints. Heart pacemakers, which help the heart to beat, are common. An artificial heart may even be invented soon.

The maglev train floats a few millimetres above its track. There is no friction because the train does not touch the track.

Scientists are inventing new and better designs all the time. But some of the best designs are already out there, just waiting to be discovered in the natural world.

Glossary

aerofoil wing shape that cuts through air and makes lift.

buoyancy being able to rise or float in water

capillarity when water rises up a tube because the water molecules are attracted to the sides of the tube.

density a measure of how closely the particles of a substance are packed together. Solids and liquids have higher density than gases.

drag the resistance to movement. The flow of air or water over a moving object slows it down.

elastic an object is said to be elastic if it goes back to its original shape after it has been stretched or squashed.

energy the ability to do work.

force a push or a pull.

friction the force that makes movement more difficult when two surfaces rub together.

gravity the attraction between two objects. Gravity holds us down on the earth.

hydraulic system a system that works by moving liquid in pipes.

hydrometer object used to measure the density of a liquid.

lever a bar that is fixed at one point. A crowbar is a lever.

lift the force of air upwards that makes an object rise into the air.

pump a machine used to move liquids from one place to another.

recoil when an elastic object returns to its original shape after squashing or stretching it is said to recoil.

resistance any force that slows movement down.

rudder object used to steer a boat or aeroplane.

stabiliser fins used by ships to stop them rolling from side to side in bad weather.

streamlining the design of a smooth, slippery shape that makes less drag.

surface tension force pulling the molecules in a liquid together, making the surface form a skin.

valve a structure that lets liquid flow only one way.

wingspan the distance between the tips of the wings.

Index